The Girl from the TAR PAPER SCHOOL

BARBARA ROSE JOHNS
AND THE ADVENT OF
THE CIVIL RIGHTS MOVEMENT

Teri Kanefield

ABRAMS BOOKS FOR YOUNG READERS · NEW YORK

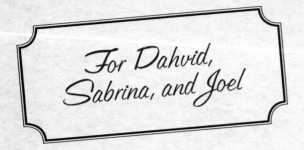

*For Dahvid,
Sabrina, and Joel*

Library of Congress Cataloging-in-Publication Data

Kanefield, Teri.
The girl from the tar paper school : Barbara Rose Johns and the
advent of the civil rights movement / by Teri Kanefield.
pages cm
Includes bibliographical references and index.
ISBN 978-1-4197-0796-4 (alk. paper)
1. Powell, Barbara Johns, 1935–1991—Juvenile literature. 2. Civil
rights movements—United States—History—20th century—
Juvenile literature. 3. Civil rights workers—United States—
Biography—Juvenile literature. 4. Women civil rights workers—
United States—Biography—Juvenile literature. 5. Segregation in
education—Virginia—History—20th century—Juvenile literature.
6. Virginia—Race relations—History—20th century—Juvenile
literature. I. Title.
E185.97.J59 K35 2013
323.092—dc23
[B]
2012040990

Text copyright © 2014 Teri Kanefield
For image credits see page 52
Book design by Maria T. Middleton

Printed and bound in China
10 9 8 7 6 5 4 3 2 1

Abrams Books for Young Readers are available at special
discounts when purchased in quantity for premiums and
promotions as well as fundraising or educational use. Special
editions can also be created to specification. For details, contact
specialsales@abramsbooks.com or the address below.

115 West 18th Street
New York, NY 10011
www.abramsbooks.com

CONTENTS

In the middle of the twentieth century, in a remote county that time had left to dawdle amid the picturebook loveliness of the Virginia countryside, a leader arose among the black people.

—PULITZER PRIZE-WINNING AUTHOR RICHARD KLUGER, FROM *SIMPLE JUSTICE*, A NATIONAL BOOK AWARD FINALIST

BARBARA JOHNS
She led pupils.

RIGHT: This photograph of Barbara appeared in the *Richmond Afro-American* in 1951 and again in 1953.

BELOW: Robert R. Moton High School students, photographed with a pennant during the 1952 homecoming events.

The Tar Paper Shack Problem

THE YEAR WAS 1950. BARBARA ROSE JOHNS WAS a fifteen-year-old high school junior with a problem to solve. Barbara and her sister, Joan, attended the Robert R. Moton High School for black students, located in the nearest town, Farmville, Virginia, fifteen miles from their farm. Her brothers, Ernest and Roderick, attended the Mary Branch Elementary School, also in Farmville.

Moton High was a squat brick building nestled in a fork of Route 15. Alongside the school were temporary classrooms built to accommodate an overflow of students. The structures were made of wood covered with a heavy paper coated with tar. The students called them chicken coops. The tar paper shacks were Barbara's problem. They didn't appear to be temporary.

When it rained, the roofs leaked. Buckets collected the dripping water. Some students sat under umbrellas so the ink on their papers wouldn't run. The makeshift classrooms, like the regular classrooms, were heated by potbellied wood stoves

Moton High School: The main brick building is in the center; the tar paper shacks are to the sides. 1952.

instead of furnaces. Students sitting near the stoves were too hot. Students sitting farther away from the stoves shivered in their coats, hats, scarves, and gloves. As a result, they frequently got sick. Teachers had to stop their lessons to stoke the fire. Smoke often eddied into the room instead of going up the chimney, causing sneezing and watery eyes.

ONE DAY, BARBARA SPOKE TO HER FAVORITE teacher, Miss Inez Davenport, about the problem of the shacks. Miss Davenport taught music at the high school. Barbara had come to know her on a personal level when she and Joan took piano lessons from her. Barbara had grown to trust her, feeling she could share her private thoughts without Miss Davenport thinking her childish.

"I'm sick and tired of it all," Barbara told her. Barbara talked about Moton's inadequacies and Farmville High's superior facilities. Farmville High, the school for white students, had modern heating, an industrial-arts shop, locker rooms, an infirmary, a cafeteria, and a real auditorium complete with sound equipment.

When Barbara finished speaking, she looked to Miss Davenport for an answer. But Miss Davenport was the type of teacher who encouraged her students to think for themselves. She believed life was like music: varied and rich, lending itself to different moods, moments, thoughts, and opinions. So instead of offering a solution, Miss Davenport asked a question: "Why don't *you* do something about it?"

Barbara turned away, disappointed. At the time, she didn't understand the importance of the question. She felt Miss Davenport had dismissed her with that reply.

ABOVE: Barbara was often described as a quiet girl, inward, intelligent, and mature. 1952.

ABOVE: Farmville High School, Prince Edward County's white high school. 1953.

ABOVE: Miss Inez Davenport, Barbara's favorite teacher. 1953.

When Barbara was in high school, segregation was legal in the United States. Segregation meant that white people and black people should attend separate schools and should, in general, be kept apart: Under segregation laws, known as the Jim Crow laws, blacks were not permitted to drink from the same water fountains as white people, play in the same parks, or enter certain public buildings.

The Constitution, the highest law in the land, says nothing specifically about segregation. However, the Fourteenth Amendment, added after the Civil War, requires that all persons be afforded equal protection of the laws. The Supreme Court has the task of interpreting the Constitution and, hence, deciding the constitutionality of any law. In an 1896 case called *Plessy v. Ferguson*, the Supreme Court declared segregation constitutional as long as separate facilities were equal.

After that case, schools throughout the country were segregated. In fact, the laws of Virginia *required* that schools be segregated.

"A Little Child Shall Lead Them"

OVER THE NEXT FEW DAYS, BARBARA SPENT TIME in the woods near her home in Darlington Heights contemplating the problem of the tar paper shacks. The Johnses' house, perched atop a slight hill, was a wood-frame structure painted white with black trim. A porch wrapped around the front. Barbara's favorite place to think was a secluded spot down the hill from the house where the woods grew thick, the underbrush dense. Sitting on a stump while her horse, Sadie Red, grazed or drank from the nearby creek, she thought about the tar paper classrooms.

As Barbara pondered the problem, her imagination ran wild, and she dreamed that a mighty man of great wealth would build the black students

of Prince Edward County a new school. She even imagined the celebration that would follow. Other times, she imagined a great storm flattening the tar paper shacks and a new building arising magically from the wreckage.

She thought about the problem as she went about her chores, chopping wood and feeding the pigs. She prayed, "God, please grant us a new school. Please let us have a warm place to stay where we won't have to keep our coats on all day. Please help us. We are your children, too."

BARBARA'S FATHER, ROBERT MELVIN JOHNS, A farmer, worked long hours in the field growing corn, soybeans, watermelon, sunflowers, and tobacco. Tobacco was his main cash crop. In 1950, however, a small tobacco farm didn't bring in much money. To help make ends meet, Barbara's mother, Violet Adele Johns, worked full time as a clerk in the Navy Department in Washington, D.C., more than 165 miles to the northeast.

ABOVE: Pictured in front of their Grandmother Croner's home are Barbara, age fifteen; Joan, age twelve; and Ernest, age nine. Not pictured is Roderick, who was six at the time. The youngest sibling, Robert, was not born until July 19, 1951. This photograph was taken in 1950.

BELOW: The entire fifteen miles of road from Farmville to the Johnses' home looks like this today, with an occasional house or farm. It has not changed much since Barbara lived there.

During the workweek, while their mother was gone, Barbara was in charge of her younger siblings and the household tasks. She rose early to help everyone get ready for school. She cleaned, cooked, and made sure all the chores were done.

One morning in October, she was so busy rushing her brothers and sister down the hill to wait for the bus that she forgot her lunch and had to run back to the house to retrieve it. In the meantime, the old bus arrived and picked up her siblings, leaving her behind. There was nothing to do but wait for someone to come along who might give her a ride. Her family lived in the Darlington Heights region, fifteen miles south of Farmville, an area consisting mostly of forests, low rolling hills, and farmland. In that part of Virginia, you could wait a long time for a car to drive by.

An hour later, she was still waiting. Down the road she saw the school bus for the white children approaching, shiny and new—and half empty—on its way to Farmville High. The bus would pass Moton High, but Barbara couldn't ride it. The bus went right by her but of course didn't stop. The injustice stung.

"Right then and there," Barbara later said, "I decided something had to be done about this inequality—but I still didn't know what."

Moton High cheerleaders. 1952.

Barbara knew that Moton High's principal and Parent Teacher Association (PTA) had been working for years to convince the all-white school board to allocate money to build a new school for black students. There had been endless delays, one excuse after another, a true bureaucratic runaround. She suspected that the school board and town officials, left to themselves, would never actually build a new school, even though the law required separate facilities to be equal. A plan took shape:

> *As I lay in my bed that night, I*
> *prayed for help. That night, whether*
> *in a dream or whether I was*
> *awake—but I felt I was awake—a*
> *plan began to formulate in my mind,*
> *a plan I felt was divinely inspired,*
> *because I hadn't been able to think*
> *of anything until then.*

Her idea was to assemble the Moton High class leaders, those she considered the crème de la crème, and with them lead a strike to protest the unfair conditions at their school.

Barbara would give a speech to inspire her classmates. They would carry signs and march in front of the school. Their strike would draw the attention of citizens of Farmville and beyond. People would hear them and sympathize. With students refusing to attend a substandard school, the school board, superintendent, and leaders of Farmville would have no choice but to grant the black students a new building.

The next morning she arose, refreshed and energized, ready to put her plan into action, confident that events would unfold as she'd imagined. After all, didn't the Bible say that "the wolf also shall dwell with the lamb . . . and *a little child shall lead them*"?

The Quiet Embrace of the Woods

BARBARA'S FAMILY HAD LIVED IN PRINCE EDWARD County for generations. Both of her parents and all four of her grandparents were born there. Her mother's family, the Spencers, and her father's family, the Johnses, attended the same Baptist church, Triumph.

Shortly after Barbara's parents were married, they moved to New York City in search of work, living in a Harlem rooming house with some of her mother's relatives. Her father did odd jobs, and her mother worked as a domestic servant.

Barbara was born in New York City on March 6, 1935. When she was fourteen months old, her parents gave up trying to scrape together a living in New York and returned to Prince Edward County.

They moved into some rooms behind a store belonging to Barbara's Uncle Vernon, her father's older brother. The store had a gas pump and a mill. On the mill was a sign: LEAVE YOUR CORN AS YOU GO TO TOWN. WHEN YOU RETURN, IT WILL BE GROUND. And another: WE GRIND CORN AS FINE AS FLOUR. Barbara's parents tended the store and mill and pumped gasoline.

But the store wasn't able to support their growing family—by then, Barbara's sister, Joan, and the oldest of her brothers, Ernest, had been born. So in 1942, Barbara's family moved to Washington, D.C., where they lived in an apartment not far from the Capitol building. Mrs. Johns found steady clerical work, and Mr. Johns took odd jobs.

When World War II broke out, Mr. Johns was drafted into the army. The resulting financial strain forced Barbara's mother to take her children back to Prince Edward County to live with her mother, Mary Spencer Croner, now remarried, for the remainder of the war.

Barbara, then seven years old, thoroughly enjoyed the train ride to Virginia, particularly because the car was full of soldiers dressed smartly in their crisp uniforms. She explained later:

*The ride on the train had been
exciting, mainly because it was my
first train ride, but mostly because
it was crowded with soldiers. I was
fascinated by all of them. They were
tall men who looked so handsome
and polished in their uniforms. I
was particularly impressed by them
because my own Daddy had been
called into the army, and though I
had not seen him in his uniform, I
imagined he must look as handsome
as these men.*

TOP: Barbara's parents in 1944.

BOTTOM: Barbara's maternal grandmother, Mary Croner, and her second husband, Robert. Circa 1950.

TOP: Grandmother Croner's house as it looks today. When Barbara and her siblings lived there, the house had a red tin roof but no electricity. Inside, it was lit with kerosene lamps; outside, with lanterns. At one time, eleven people lived there.

BOTTOM: Barbara attended elementary school in this one-room schoolhouse located near her Grandmother Croner's house. The schoolhouse also served as the black community's children's Sunday school. Early on Sunday mornings, Mary Croner sent her grandchildren to light the potbellied stove for warmth. 1937.

AFTER THE CHILDREN WERE SETTLED ON THEIR grandmother's farm, Mrs. Johns returned to Washington, D.C., to live with her sister and work in the city.

Mary Croner and her second husband were patient, sturdy, hardworking farmers. Barbara adjusted readily to the routine of the farm. She seldom got the chance to sit down before hearing her grandmother call "Barbree!"—her grandmother's pet name for her. Barbara would run to feed the chickens, or gather the eggs, or pick up chips for the wood stove, or fetch a bucket of fresh water from the spring—whatever chore was needed. Mary Croner approved of her serious and hardworking granddaughter. "She didn't have a lot of put-on airs about her," Mary said. "She was a country girl, not some flirty thing worrying about clothes."

Barbara enrolled in a one-room school, which also served as a Sunday school, set in a patch of pine not far from her grandmother's home. First through seventh grades were taught in the single room. After elementary school, students went to the high school.

In school and at home, Barbara thrived. She later remembered those years as happy ones.

Sometimes at night Barbara and Joan slipped

out of bed and listened at the door while the adults talked of the old days. They heard about life during slave times, and recent lynchings. These stories frightened Joan and convinced her she'd be killed if she angered a white person, but they raised Barbara's fighting spirit.

When Mr. Johns returned home on temporary leave from the army, he moved his children to the home of his mother, Sallie Johns. Sallie didn't farm, and she lived in a smaller house, so there were fewer chores and more time for reading and writing and studying.

Sallie Johns was an intelligent, outspoken woman who admired those traits in others. She argued good-naturedly, but nevertheless she argued about everything from when the war would end to how much sugar a person should put in a cup of coffee. What impressed Barbara about her grandmother was her fearlessness: Sallie Johns was not the slightest bit subservient to whites.

Barbara's Uncle Vernon was the most spirited and dynamic member of the Johns family—perhaps one of the most spirited and perplexing citizens in Prince Edward County's history. Hailed as brilliant—and a dangerous firebrand—Reverend Vernon Johns was an ordained Baptist minister, educated at Virginia Union in Richmond,

Reverend Vernon Johns at the pulpit, circa late 1950s.

Oberlin College in Ohio, and Virginia Theological Seminary in Lynchburg. His method was to shock and anger. For example, one of his sermons was titled, "It Is Safe to Murder Negroes." He offended blacks when he chided them for docility and ignorance. He offended whites when he denounced lynching as immoral. Barbara thought he towered intellectually over the entire county, black and white.

During those years, Vernon's wife, Altona—another music teacher at Moton High—and their children were also living in the home of Sallie Johns. Reverend Johns was in and out, often gone for months at a time, lecturing at colleges and giving sermons. When he was home, he preached locally and wrote for various periodicals.

Reverend Johns made sure his children and his nieces and nephews read the serious and weighty books he kept in the house. He quizzed them regularly, particularly about black history. He required the children to read the encyclopedia, starting with *A* and working their way to *Z*.

Barbara, an avid reader, eagerly read such books as *The Postman Always Rings Twice* and *The War of the Worlds* and denser volumes such as *Up from Slavery* and *Native Son*. However, she didn't care for her uncle's imposed reading, so sometimes while she was supposed to be reading the encyclopedia, she inserted *Betty and Veronica* comic books between the pages and read those instead.

WORLD WAR II ENDED WHEN BARBARA WAS ten. Her father returned from Europe, and her mother came home from Washington. Reverend Johns, at about this time, moved his own family to Montgomery, Alabama, where he became pastor of the Dexter Avenue Baptist Church.

While Barbara's father built a new house and barn, the family went back to living in the rooms behind Reverend Vernon's store. In the living room behind the store, the fireplace was flanked by two bookcases reaching to the ceiling, filled with books. Barbara, her siblings, and her parents spent pleasant evenings reading by the fire. During the day, they pumped gasoline, tended the mill, and waited on customers in the store.

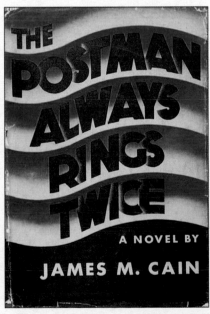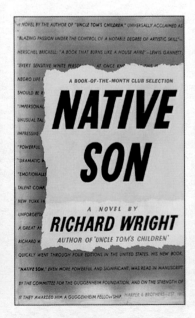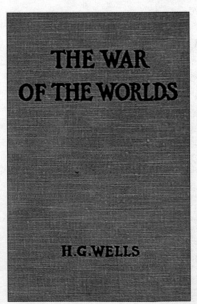

A few of the books Barbara enjoyed as a child.

ABOVE: Farmville's only hotel, the State Theater, and the drugstore lunch counter were for whites only. Blacks could only enter the hotel as workers. Clothing stores permitted black shoppers to make purchases but not to try on clothes. This image is from a postcard, circa 1950.

OPPOSITE: John Watson and two Moton High girls. 1952.

White people in the South often called blacks "Uncle" and "Aunt" instead of titles of respect such as "Mr." or "Mrs." This forced familiarity dated back to slave days and was used purposely to degrade them.

The store was frequented by blacks and whites. One white girl often came into the store with her father. She and Barbara sat together and talked, and Barbara thought her beautiful. One day, Barbara saw the girl in the five-and-ten-cent store in Farmville and greeted her, but the girl coolly turned away. Barbara seethed, fully aware she'd been snubbed because of her race.

Barbara was also irritated when white customers called her father "Uncle Robert." Once she spoke up and said, "Why are you calling him Uncle? He is not your uncle." Her words shocked her sister and elders. Barbara had been raised to be respectful to all adults, and in the 1950s in rural Virginia, black children simply did not speak to whites that way. Family members observed—with pride and apprehension—that Barbara seemed to be taking after her Uncle Vernon.

WHEN THE JOHNSES' NEW FAMILY HOME IN DARlington Heights was finished, with much excitement Barbara, her parents, and her siblings moved in. The boys shared a first-floor bedroom across from their parents' room. Barbara and Joan shared a second-floor attic room and a full-size bed. Sometimes after they were supposed to be asleep, the girls hid under the blankets with flashlights to read.

Shortly after they were settled in their new home, Barbara befriended a white girl who lived across the road. The girl's parents, though, forbade their daughter to associate with nonwhites, so the two girls hid their friendship, sneaking off to play in the woods. By the time Barbara was in high school, the white family had moved away.

As Barbara became a teenager, she took to spending time alone in the woods, in her place near the creek, where she meditated and looked inward. As she later explained,

I roamed throughout the woods, wrapping myself in its quiet embraces, listening only to the sounds of the birds, the scattering of the squirrels, rabbits, and other small creatures underfoot. Occasionally a startled deer would leap hurriedly away, or a brace of quail would take flight, or some other small creature would scurry about—but mostly it was quiet and peaceful.

The Time Has Come

THE MORNING AFTER BARBARA THOUGHT OF THE idea for a strike, she arrived at school eager to put her plan into action. She approached about a half dozen class leaders. Among these were the twins John and Carrie Stokes, and John Watson. Carrie was president of the 1951 graduating class. John Stokes was vice president, active on the debate team and in New Farmers of America. John Watson was a member of the football team, editor-in-chief of the school newspaper, and a member of the Moton High Progressive Business Club. She told this select group her idea and arranged a meeting time and place.

They held their initial meeting in October 1950, on the cinder block bleachers facing the athletic field. Barbara pointed out to the group that their parents and teachers had made almost no progress in replacing their temporary classrooms. She said it was time for the students to take the lead. The others agreed. They, too, were tired of attending school in tar paper shacks.

The group decided that the best time to strike would be late in the spring, to create an urgent situation: With students on strike, there could be no finals or graduation. Until then, the group would attend school board meetings and closely monitor any developments. In a few months they would meet again to assess if there had been any progress on a new high school.

At the February 1951 school board meeting, the members of the school board told the Moton High PTA that the Farmville Board of Supervisors had given permission to purchase a site for a new high school for black students. The members of the school board—all of them white—also told the Moton High students, parents, and teachers not to bother coming to future meetings. They would be informed of any new developments.

As of April, nothing had changed. There was no sign of a new building in the works. The students were ready to go on strike.

OPPOSITE: The school's athletic field as it looked when Barbara attended Moton High. 1952.

FAR LEFT: Edwilda Allen (left) and Joan Johns (right). Edwilda Allen was the eighth-grade representative during the strike. 1953.

LEFT: Principal Boyd Jones. 1951.

The group handpicked other leaders to join them, bringing in students who lived in different areas and who were in different age groups, so the strike would have a wide base of support.

Edwilda Allen, the eighth-grade representative, remembers sitting outside with Barbara near the athletic field. "Barbara told me the plan," Edwilda said, "and explained what everyone was going to do." Edwilda was taken by Barbara's idea but found it hard to believe the plan would work and that everyone would follow her. "We were taught to be obedient and respectful, and there she was, asking us to be disobedient. It was shocking."

Complete secrecy was vital. Parents or teachers suspected of participating in, or even tacitly allowing, the strike could lose their jobs—or worse. Barbara kept the secret from her own parents. Her father, she felt, was too busy plowing and planting and harvesting to bother with her plan, which he would probably consider foolish. He would never give her permission to go on strike, but he wouldn't be able to stop her. So why bother telling him? God, she felt, had given her the idea. Her task was to follow through.

She kept the secret from her sister as well. Joan, meek and easily frightened, would be so scared by the idea, she might be tempted to tell their parents.

To get Principal Boyd Jones away from the school, the students decided someone should leave campus, call him, and tell him some of his students were making trouble downtown. They knew that the principal would believe this, because it had happened before. After one such incident, he'd obtained a promise from the white business owners that if any of his students made trouble in town during school hours, the business owners would call him instead of the police so he could take care of it.

Barbara told John Watson he should be the one to make the call. His family, after all, was one of the few black families with a telephone. Moreover, nobody would be able to eavesdrop, because his family had a private phone instead of a shared, or party, phone. Also, the Watsons lived on Hill Street, one of three possible routes Principal Jones could take downtown, and someone had to be stationed along each route to watch and make sure the principal swallowed the bait and left the school.

John Watson didn't want to be the one to make the call. He felt he had a distinctive voice and didn't think he could impersonate an older white man. Barbara encouraged him, suggesting he put a handkerchief over the phone's mouthpiece.

They selected the day and time for the strike: eleven o'clock, the usual time for assemblies, on Monday, April 23, 1951.

WHENEVER PRINCIPAL JONES CALLED AN ASSEM-bly, he would write notes signed with his initial, J. The notes went onto clipboards, and certain girls hand delivered them to the teachers.

In preparation for the strike, Barbara wrote similar notes and signed them with a J. The task of taking the notes to the classrooms was given to the girls who ordinarily delivered them.

At the appointed time, John Watson and a few others left the school and positioned themselves in various places to watch for the principal. Just before 11:00 A.M., John Watson telephoned the principal's office and, disguising his voice, convinced Principal Jones that some of his students were causing trouble downtown.

Principal Jones, predictably, left in a hurry. The moment he was gone, the students swung into action. The girls delivered the notes, and Barbara waited on the stage in the auditorium behind the curtain.

The main school building was built in wings leading from the auditorium. To get from one classroom to another, or from the library to a classroom, or from the principal's office to anywhere else, you had to pass through the auditorium. Soon came the pounding of feet and scraping of chairs as 450 students and their teachers flocked to the auditorium and sat in folding metal chairs.

When the purple and gold curtain went up, and the assembled students saw Barbara at the rostrum instead of Principal Jones, there was surprise

These two photographs, one of Moton High's auditorium (left) and the other of Farmville High's (below), show the disparity between the two schools. 1952.

and hubbub. Joan, sitting in the front row, was shocked. Knowing something highly irregular was happening, she cowered and hunched down in her chair.

Barbara announced that the assembly was for students only, so she'd be obliged if the teachers would please leave. A few teachers left willingly. Others had to be persuaded to leave.

Barbara gave a speech that students later described as electrifying and inspiring. She talked about the appalling conditions at their school and the inability of the PTA and others to secure better facilities. She said the students had the right to *equal* facilities, and it was clear that nothing would

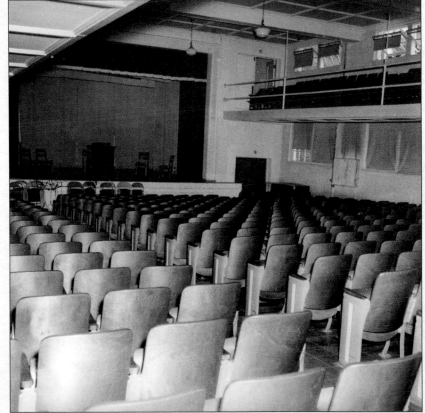

happen unless the students banded together and took action.

Later, Barbara couldn't recall her exact words, but one classmate remembered her saying, "Are we going to just accept these conditions? Or are we going to do something about it?"

Before Barbara delivered this speech, many of her classmates, who saw her as reserved and something of a loner, hardly knew who she was. Her riveting speech, therefore, took many by surprise. "After that speech," one student reflected later, "*everyone* knew who she was."

"She put into words what needed to be said," recalled another student. "I was glad someone had the courage to stand up and say it."

Unbeknownst to those in the auditorium, at the start of the assembly, one student left school and ran toward town, shouting that a riot had broken out. The rumor of a riot quickly spread. Among the first to hear the rumor was John and Carrie Stokes's mother, who startled her children by appearing in the auditorium doorway and demanding to know what was going on. Seeing that the assembly was orderly, however, she left.

Before long, Principal Jones, having figured out that he'd been sent on a wild-goose chase, rushed into the auditorium. Seeing what was afoot, he urged the students to return to class. He told them this sort of action would not solve their problems. He said progress was being made with the school board, so they must be patient.

Barbara asked Mr. Jones to go back to his office. After more discussion, he left, as distressed as when he had entered. Barbara was now in command of the school!

The students all began talking at once, shouting questions at Barbara, demanding to know how her plan would work. To maintain order, Barbara took off a shoe and hit the rostrum with it for attention. When she got silence, she explained why a strike was necessary and assured her classmates that nobody would be punished if they all stuck together. "The jail isn't big enough for all of us," she said.

She gave instructions: Everyone was to follow her out of the building. They must remain on school grounds. They could carry handmade signs and march in an orderly manner in front of the school, or they could sit inside quietly at their desks—but they were not to open their books or engage in lessons.

Others were fearful, but Barbara was not.

She walked out of the school building, and all the students followed her.

Stick with Us

WHEN REVEREND L. FRANCIS GRIFFIN RECEIVED a phone call from one of the students at the high school, he'd already heard rumors in town of what was afoot. The caller asked him to come to the school to meet with the students. He went right away.

Reverend Griffin was pastor at the First Baptist Church on Main Street in Farmville. He was also active on the Moton High PTA, so he shared the students' frustrations over the tar paper shacks. He was a large, beefy, sleepy-eyed man who moved slowly. His appearance was deceiving: His gait was slow but his mind sharp, his wit caustic.

It wouldn't have been hard for the students to guess that Reverend Griffin would be among the adults sympathetic to their strike. He was president of the local chapter of the National Association for the Advancement of Colored People (NAACP). In fact, there *was* a local chapter only because he had single-handedly canvassed the county and obtained the fifty signatures needed. Finding fifty people willing to sign on the line in a county like Prince Edward had not been easy. The white population frowned upon the organization and its agenda. And the black population was, in Griffith's view and the view of Barbara's Uncle Vernon, too beaten-down, timid, and long-suffering to be capable of bold action.

Reverend Griffin, like Barbara's uncle, believed prayer alone would not change the world. Nor would begging. He found guidance in the biblical story of what had happened when Moses begged Pharaoh to reduce the Israelites' quota of brick production—the plea only made matters worse. The lesson for Griffin was that begging was not the way to gain relief from oppression.

The Reverend arrived at the high school to find the students picketing. The students who had summoned him were in a closed-door meeting in the library. He was ushered in to join them. The students had a single question for him. One boy was dissenting, insisting they get permission from their parents before proceeding. Others believed that getting permission would embroil their parents and possibly put them in danger. What did the Reverend think?

Reverend Griffin advised the students to vote among themselves and follow the rule of the majority. The group followed his advice, the dissenting boy was outvoted, and the strike remained in student hands. Later, Griffin was accused of instigating the strike. He denied any prior knowledge of the strike but freely admitted to doing all he could to help, once the students had taken action.

After the meeting in the library, Barbara called the NAACP's Richmond office and asked for lawyers to come to Farmville to help the students. Oliver Hill, the NAACP lawyer who took the call, told her to end the strike and go back to school. Barbara refused and insisted he come to Farmville right away. Hill, who did not consider the matter serious enough, told Barbara she could write him a letter.

That afternoon, Barbara and Carrie Stokes composed a letter, which Carrie typed:

Gentlemen:

We hate to impose as we are doing, but under the circumstances that we are facing, we have to ask for your help.

Due to the fact that the facilities and building in the name of Robert R. Moton High School are inadequate, we understand that your help is available to us. This morning, April 23, 1951, the students refused to attend classes under the circumstances. You know that this is a very serious matter because we are out of school, there are seniors to be graduated and it can't be done by staying at home. Please we beg you to come down at the first of this week. If possible, Wednesday, April 25, between nine A.M. and three P.M.

We will provide a place for you to stay.

We will go into detail when you arrive.

The two girls signed and mailed the letter that afternoon.

Barbara and the others also wanted to meet with T. J. McIlwaine, the white superintendent of Prince Edward County schools. They wished to present their demands and negotiate with him, but Mr. McIlwaine refused to see them. He viewed the strike as a breach of discipline and held Principal Jones responsible for not squelching the protest immediately.

AT THE USUAL TIME, BARBARA AND HER SIBLINGS rode the bus home. That evening, Barbara told her parents about the strike. They were bewildered and frightened—but sympathetic and supportive. Later, her father said, "I'm not surprised by anything Barbara does."

Barbara went to visit Mary Croner. "Grandma," she said, "I walked out of school this morning and carried four hundred and fifty students with me."

Those words took her grandmother's breath away. "You reckon you done the right thing?" she asked.

"I believe so," Barbara said. "Stick with us."

In 1935, the NAACP launched a legal campaign to better school conditions for black children in the South. The strategy was to bring lawsuits demonstrating that schools were not equal and, hence, were illegal. The idea was that if the South had to spend the money necessary to create two separate but equal school districts, citizens would awaken to the economic waste and folly of two separate systems. The NAACP, however, was unprepared for the white community's resistance to spending money on black schools. In 1950, after fifteen years of such lawsuits—including obtaining federal court orders that local school boards refused to follow—school facilities remained, in many cases, as unequal as those in Farmville.

Moton High Library. 1952.

ABOVE: Mr. McIlwaine, superintendent of Prince Edward County schools. 1952.

BELOW: Main Street, Farmville. 1943.

RIGHT: The Prince Edward County Courthouse looks the same today as it did in 1951, with the exception of the Light of Reconciliation, the illumination of the bell tower, dedicated to Barbara and her classmates.

Main Street, looking North, Farmville, Va.

Reaching for the Moon

ON THE SECOND DAY OF THE STRIKE, SUPERINtendent McIlwaine still refused to come to Moton High to meet with the students, so a small group that included the members of the strike planning committee walked downtown to his office. Barbara felt self-conscious as white people gathered to watch them walk past. She pretended not to notice or mind the staring and whispering.

There wasn't room for everyone in Mr. McIlwaine's office, so the group trooped to the county courthouse and met upstairs in the courtroom.

Mr. McIlwaine, a smallish man with a nervous habit of looking away when people talked to him, sat behind the rail where lawyers would normally sit. A man with a clipboard went around to each student, writing down the student's name and the names of his or her parents. The intention was to intimidate the students, and the act of taking down their parents' names did, in fact, frighten many of them.

Barbara, as spokesperson for the group, did most of the talking. Among her questions was why Moton High students couldn't simply attend school with the whites. Mr. McIlwaine explained that mixing races in schools was against Virginia law. He went on to say that a new building was in the works, and they would have to be patient. He said that most of the taxes were paid by whites, so, naturally, the white school was better funded. Without looking the students in the eye, he also said Moton High was as good as Farmville High.

When the students remained firm, Mr. McIlwaine resorted to threats: If they didn't end the strike immediately, their parents and teachers would lose their jobs or perhaps go to jail.

After speaking with the students, the superintendent was convinced the strike was a "put-up job" instigated by adults, with the students parroting words they had been given. He also believed that Principal Jones had planted students downtown to make trouble so he'd have an excuse to leave and allow the students to take over the school.

ON WEDNESDAY MORNING, THE THIRD DAY OF the strike, Reverend Griffin told the students the NAACP lawyers had come to meet with them. The lawyers had taken a detour to Farmville en route to an appointment farther south. All students in attendance at Moton High that day walked the mile to Reverend Griffin's church.

The meeting was held in the church basement. Reverend Griffin introduced the two lawyers, Oliver Hill and Spottswood Robinson.

The lawyers stunned the students by telling them to return to class. Quite simply, Mr. Hill and Mr. Robinson believed that a rural backwater like Prince Edward County was not the place to wage a legal battle over school facilities. Such a battle would have a better chance in the cities, where the white community was less resistant to change.

r. Robinson and Mr. Hill understood—even if the students did not—how the white population of Prince Edward County was likely to react to a demand for integration. Recently Mr. Robinson had been in Cumberland County, just north of Prince Edward County, where he tried to get the school board to replace tar paper shack classrooms much like those at Moton High. A school board official told him, "We'd like to help you fellas, but you're pushing too fast, and we just don't have enough money." Mr. Robinson said, "Look, I know how you could do it overnight—all you have to do is let the colored kids into Cumberland High School." At which point one of the school board members leaped to his feet and shouted, "The first little black son of a b——— that comes down the road to set foot in that school, I'll take my shotgun and blow his brains out."

ABOVE: NAACP representatives Oliver Hill (left) and Spottswood Robinson (right). 1948.

OPPOSITE: Students arriving by bus in front of the tar paper shacks. 1953.

But the students refused to abandon their strike. They argued respectfully, but they argued— so the lawyers debated with them. What would the students do if the school board absolutely refused to build them a new school? *We will stay out of school indefinitely*, they said. What if the officials enforced the truancy laws? *No jail is big enough for all of us*.

The students would not be dissuaded. The lawyers, who did not have the heart to give them a flat-out no, did what they considered the equivalent: They explained they were no longer using their resources to bring lawsuits for the purpose of obtaining equal facilities. Their strategy now was to work toward ending segregation itself. They would work with the students only if their parents were solidly behind them, and only if the view was to end segregation in Prince Edward County.

Barbara, listening, felt awed by the enormity of what the lawyers were proposing. Demanding full integration, which was contrary to existing law, seemed to her like reaching for the moon.

ON THE FOURTH DAY OF THE STRIKE, SUPERINTENdent McIlwaine delivered a blow: He withdrew Moton High's school buses. Without buses, the majority of students could not easily get to school. The students met this challenge by borrowing cars and trucks, recruiting drivers, and organizing car

pools. They succeeded in bringing enough students to school for the public protest to continue.

After school that fourth day, the students canvassed the county, carrying petitions, collecting signatures, and asking adults in the black community for support. They spread the word that there would be a mass meeting that night in the First Baptist Church for the PTA and parents interested in learning more about a possible lawsuit.

One thousand people showed up at the meeting held in the church—one quarter of the entire black population of the county. The members of the school board had also been invited, but not a single white person attended.

Lester Banks, executive secretary of the Virginia State Conference, NAACP. Circa 1950.

Lester Banks, executive secretary of the Virginia State Conference of the NAACP, conducted the meeting in the absence of Spottswood Robinson and Oliver Hill, who had to be elsewhere. He praised the courage of the students in striking for a new school building and said, "The problem is that a new colored high school will not bring you equality, even if it is built brick for brick, cement for cement, like the white school. . . . When colored people are separated, we're stamped with a brand of inferiority. As long as we accept separate schools, we accept a caste system that says we're unfit to sit beside whites. This segregation must not be allowed to continue."

When he finished speaking, there was a thunder of applause.

Contrary to all expectations, the Moton High parents voted unanimously to demand integration. The population that, in the words of Vernon Johns, was "too docile and long-suffering to act decisively" acted decisively that evening.

"We met whatever obstacle we were given, no matter how difficult," John Watson said later. The students' explanation for such unexpected success was that God was working with them.

Pupil Lashes Out at Principal

THE NEXT DAY, AN EDITORIAL IN THE *FARMVILLE Herald* denounced the strike as "ill advised" and "student-inspired mass-hookie." A mocking letter to the editor suggested that the students were looking for a chance to play outside instead of studying. The *Richmond Times* ran an insignificant article buried on the seventh page of the paper.

Though these newspapers failed to take the strike seriously, a second meeting was held the

Ill Advised Move

For three days all members of the student body of Robert R. Morton High School in Farmville have absented themselves from the classrooms. The teachers have been present to teach, the school busses have operated — these facilities and services have been supplied at considerable cost by the county. The purpose of the apparently student-inspired mass hookie is to hasten the construction of a new school building, which is needed and is under consideration by the county school board. Temporary classrooms were built two years ago to meet a pressing need, until plans and arrangements could be made adequately to meet the needs.

The ill advised student action is to be regretted. It will not and should not influence the present plan from the authorities. To us it is the sign of the times. It might be the product of the present system of education, it might result from the lack of discipline so obvious in the home, the church, the school, and in everyday philosophy of living. It is not characteristic of the people of Southside Virginia and certainly not in keeping with the principles taught by the great educator Robert R. Moton, a native of this area, for whom the school is named. It is an ill-advised tactic of immature youth and should be so considered.

LEFT: **ILL ADVISED MOVE,** an editorial claims in the *Farmville Herald*, April 25, 1951.

BELOW: Over one thousand people attended the second meeting with the NAACP lawyers at the First Baptist Church on May 3, 1951.

Students gather around the burned cross on Moton High school grounds. 1951.

following week on Thursday, May 3, 1951, again at the First Baptist Church in Farmville. This time Mr. Hill and Mr. Robinson were present.

This time even more than one thousand people attended, leaving standing room only for many. The meeting opened with the singing of "My Country, 'Tis of Thee." Mr. Robinson, in a stirring speech, said the students could return to class once the papers demanding desegregation were filed. "They all came out together, and we want them all to go back together."

People shouted, "Amen!" Cheers rang out, and the church was shaken by the stomping of feet.

Joseph Pervall, a former principal of Moton High—a man strongly opposed to a suit for desegregation—stood up and shouted, "I was under the impression the pupils were striking for a new building. You are pulling a heavy load, Mr. Robinson, coming down here to a country town like Farmville and trying to take it over on a nonsegregated basis!"

Arguing between Mr. Pervall and the NAACP lawyers followed.

Barbara then went calmly to the podium, her eyes sharply focused on the crowd. What she said, and how she said it, sent waves of shock and pride through the assembly. In a ringing voice, she said, "Don't let Mr. Charlie, Mr. Tommy, or Mr. Pervall stop you from backing us! Don't let any Tom, Dick, or Harry Pervall stop you from supporting us!" She pleaded with the adults to support the students in their demand for equal treatment.

When Barbara finished speaking, there was thundering applause. She returned to her family and received proud hugs from her parents.

The Moton High parents and students had by now grown accustomed to this fiery and outspoken side of the girl many had previously viewed as reserved and inward. The newspaper reporter from the *Richmond Afro-American*, though, must have been startled, because the next issue of his newspaper ran the headline PUPIL LASHES OUT AT PRINCIPAL. The article said that when the "little girl with sun-kissed colored skin" directed her comments to her former principal, "there were tears in some eyes as these grownups looked at this courageous pupil, unafraid to speak her mind."

The final speaker was Reverend Griffin, who proclaimed, "Anyone who would not back these children after they stepped out on a limb is not a man. Anybody here who won't fight against racial prejudice is not a man."

The meeting ended with the crowd lifting their voices and singing "God Bless America."

ON SATURDAY, TWO DAYS LATER, A CROSS WAS burned in front of the high school. News of the burning cross spread through town. Several Moton High students gathered around the cross, which

Cross burning, or cross lighting, is a practice associated with the Ku Klux Klan, an organization dedicated to the idea of white supremacy. In the mid-twentieth century, Klan members often wore white robes and masks to hide their identities. In an attempt to frighten blacks and keep them from demanding their rights, these masked men committed acts of violence against blacks for alleged infractions. The violence included murder, shooting into houses, and burning homes.

was about eight feet tall and wrapped in a sheet burned to fragments.

John Stokes and a group of other students drove out to Barbara's home to tell her about it. She tried to calm them, suggesting that some teenagers had probably pulled a prank. For those unable to dismiss the burning cross as insignificant, however, it must have come as a somber warning.

A Lawsuit Is Filed— and the Troubles Begin

ON MONDAY, MAY 7, 1951—TWO WEEKS AFTER THE strike began—the NAACP filed a petition with the Prince Edward County school board demanding integration of the schools. That same day, the Moton High students ended their strike and returned to class.

Predictably, the Prince Edward County school board rejected the petition, so, on May 23, the NAACP filed a lawsuit in federal court alleging that segregation was unconstitutional.

The school board blamed Principal Boyd Jones for the strike and lawsuit and refused to renew his contract. As of the end of that school year, he had no job. The school board brought in a new principal from out of town.

Barbara's family faced hardships as well. Local stores and banks denied credit to her family and others involved in the lawsuit so they could not borrow money for goods such as groceries. A farmer with a small plot of land needs credit to survive from the time crops are planted until they are harvested and sold. Barbara's parents found it harder to make ends meet.

That summer, about the time Barbara's youngest brother, Robert, was born, a threat was made against Barbara's life. Her parents never told anyone the details, so nobody knows exactly what was said. However, her parents were so deeply

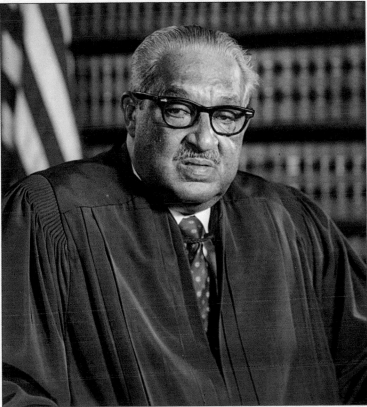

frightened that they sent Barbara to live with her Uncle Vernon and his family in Montgomery, Alabama.

The following spring, in 1952, Barbara finished high school in Montgomery—far from her friends, parents, and siblings. That autumn she enrolled at Spelman College in Atlanta, Georgia.

THE CASE OF THE MOTON HIGH STUDENTS against the school board of Prince Edward County went all the way to the United States Supreme Court, where it was joined with four similar cases from Kansas, South Carolina, Delaware, and Washington, D.C. The consolidated case was called *Brown v. Board of Education* after Oliver Brown, father of Linda Brown, a student from Kansas. The plaintiffs were represented by Thurgood Marshall.

OPPOSITE: In 1952, Barbara graduated from the Alabama State Laboratory High School in Montgomery, a school of secondary education set up by the Alabama State Teachers College for Negroes.

ABOVE: Spelman College as it appeared when Barbara enrolled. Founded in Atlanta in 1881, Spelman College today remains a premier liberal arts college for black women.

LEFT: As chief counsel of the NAACP, Thurgood Marshall argued the case of *Brown v. Board of Education* before the Supreme Court. He later became the first black person to serve as a justice on the Supreme Court, after his nomination in 1967 by President Lyndon Johnson.

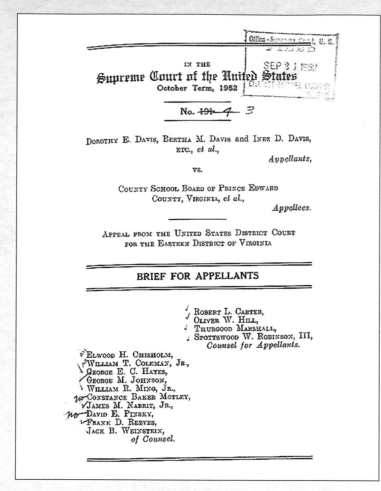

IN THE
Supreme Court of the United States
October Term, 1952

No. ~~191~~ ~~4~~ 3

DOROTHY E. DAVIS, BERTHA M. DAVIS and INEZ D. DAVIS,
ETC., et al.,
Appellants,

vs.

COUNTY SCHOOL BOARD OF PRINCE EDWARD
COUNTY, VIRGINIA, et al.,
Appellees.

APPEAL FROM THE UNITED STATES DISTRICT COURT
FOR THE EASTERN DISTRICT OF VIRGINIA

BRIEF FOR APPELLANTS

ROBERT L. CARTER,
OLIVER W. HILL,
THURGOOD MARSHALL,
SPOTTSWOOD W. ROBINSON, III,
Counsel for Appellants.

ELWOOD H. CHISHOLM,
WILLIAM T. COLEMAN, JR.,
GEORGE E. C. HAYES,
GEORGE M. JOHNSON,
WILLIAM R. MING, JR.,
CONSTANCE BAKER MOTLEY,
JAMES M. NABRIT, JR.,
DAVID E. PINSKY,
FRANK D. REEVES,
JACK B. WEINSTEIN,
of Counsel.

ABOVE: The cover page of the brief (a document describing the clients' case) filed with the United States Supreme Court on behalf of the Moton High students.

OPPOSITE: After the Prince Edward Academy was established, money was found to build the new private school, and soon construction began. Since 1985, the Prince Edward Academy—known today as the Fuqua School—has welcomed students of all races. 1961.

On May 17, 1954—three years after the strike at Moton High—the United States Supreme Court rendered its decision in *Brown v. Board of Education*, declaring segregation in schools unconstitutional. Crediting the NAACP argument that "separate but equal" can never be equal, the court specifically stated, "In the field of public education, the doctrine 'separate but equal' has no place."

Barbara was attending Spelman College when the Court made its ruling. Joan, still in high school, talked with her sister on the phone about the decision. "Barbara was so excited, she shouted with happiness," Joan recalled.

SHORTLY AFTER *BROWN V. BOARD OF EDUCATION* was decided, the Johnses' home in Darlington Heights burned down. At the time of the fire, Joan and her parents were in Washington, D.C., visiting relatives. Barbara's brothers, who were staying with their grandmother, Mary Croner, were awakened during the night and told the family home was burning. From the distance they could see the flames. They arrived with their grandmother and her husband to find the entire house and all its contents destroyed. The family was never able to find out how the fire started, but under the circumstances they suspected arson.

For a while, Barbara's parents and siblings returned to Prince Edward County and lived with Mary Croner. Mr. Johns—without any credit in town—could not rebuild the house in Darlington Heights or keep the farm running, so Barbara's family moved to Washington, D.C.

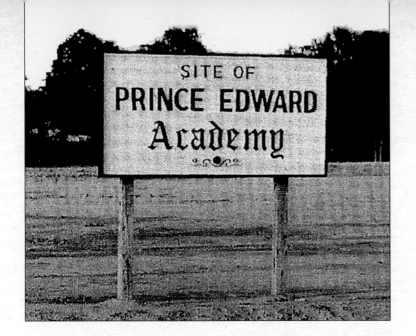

The Lost Generation

EVEN AFTER THE SUPREME COURT'S RULING IN *Brown v. Board of Education*, school systems throughout the country refused to integrate, among them the Prince Edward County public schools.

In 1959, the Federal District Court ordered Prince Edward County to desegregate. To avoid integration, the school board shut down all public schools and ordered the superintendent to change the schools' locks and keep the keys in the school board office.

The county quickly formed a private school, the Prince Edward Academy, funded by state-approved tuition grants and private donations. Only white children were enrolled in the Prince Edward Academy, so their education continued uninterrupted. Black children had no school. Black teachers lost their jobs and had to leave the county.

The black children of Prince Edward County were unable to attend school between 1959 and 1964. As a result, many of those without family resources or who were too young to leave the county and attend school elsewhere grew up illiterate. The denial of any education wreaked havoc on these children and their families for generations to come.

Almost fourteen years after Barbara led her strike, the Supreme Court ruled that closing the Prince Edward County public schools violated the Fourteenth Amendment by denying black children equal protection of the laws. Prince Edward County was ordered to reopen its schools, but because the county avoided putting money into public schools, and because initially whites refused to attend them, it was not until the 1980s that Prince Edward County schools were fully integrated and funded adequately enough so *all* children in the county could be educated.

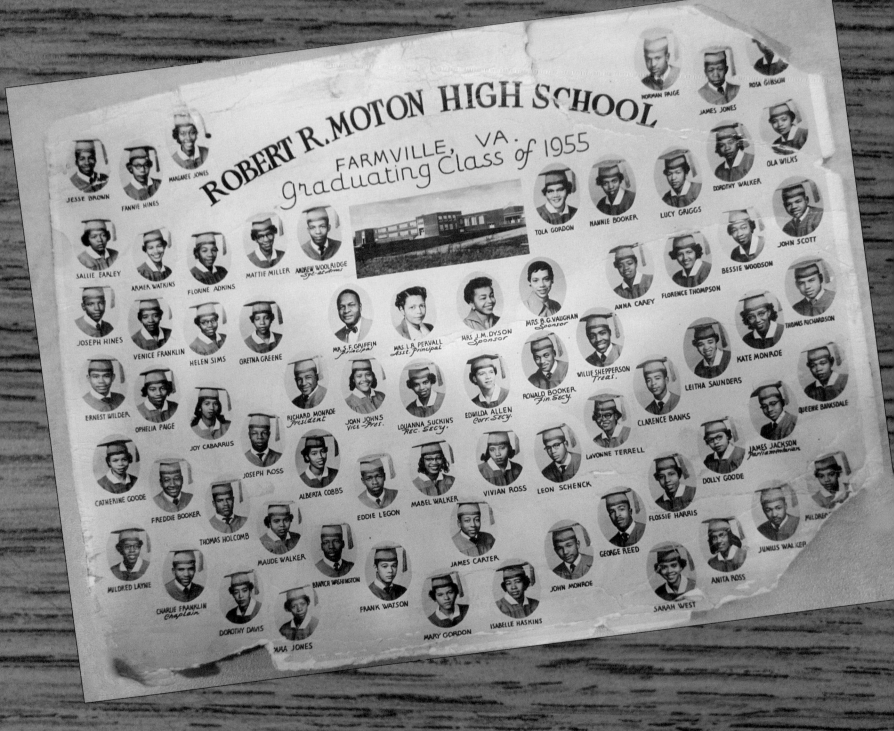

ROBERT R. MOTON HIGH SCHOOL
FARMVILLE, VA.
Graduating Class of 1955

NORMAN PAIGE
JAMES JONES
ROSA GIBSON

JESSE BROWN
FANNIE HINES
MARGAREE JONES

OLA WILKS

TOLA GORDON
NANNIE BOOKER
LUCY GRIGGS
DOROTHY WALKER

SALLIE EARLEY
ARMER WATKINS
FLORINE ADKINS
MATTIE MILLER
ANDREW WOOLRIDGE
Sgt-at-Arms

JOHN SCOTT

BESSIE WOODSON

ANNA CAREY
FLORENCE THOMPSON

JOSEPH HINES
VENICE FRANKLIN
HELEN SIMS
GRETNA GREENE
MR. S.F. GRIFFIN
Principal
MRS. L.R. PERVALL
Asst. Principal
MRS. J.M. DYSON
Sponsor
MRS. B.G. VAUGHAN
Sponsor

THOMAS RICHARDSON

KATE MONROE

ERNEST WILDER
OPHELIA PAIGE
RICHARD MONROE
President
JOAN JOHNS
Vice-Pres.
LOUANNA SUCKINS
Rec. Secy.
EDWILDA ALLEN
Corr. Secy.
RONALD BOOKER
Fin. Secy.
WILLIE SHEPPERSON
Treas.
LEITHA SAUNDERS

QUEENIE BANKSDALE

JOY CABARRUS
CLARENCE BANKS

JAMES JACKSON
Parliamentarian

CATHERINE GOODE
JOSEPH ROSS
ALBERTA COBBS
MABEL WALKER
VIVIAN ROSS
LEON SCHENCK
LaVONNE TERRELL
DOLLY GOODE

FREDDIE BOOKER
EDDIE LEGON

FLOSSIE HARRIS

MILDRED

THOMAS HOLCOMB
MAUDE WALKER
JAMES CARTER
GEORGE REED

JUNIUS WALKER

MILDRED LAYNE
CHARLIE FRANKLIN
Chaplain
BRANCH WASHINGTON
FRANK WATSON
JOHN MONROE
ANITA ROSS

DOROTHY DAVIS
MARY GORDON
ISABELLE HASKINS
SARAH WEST

JONES

"Nothing Is So Strong as Gentleness, Nothing So Gentle as Strength."

OPPOSITE: Graduates of the class of 1955, Moton High School. These students participated in the strike during their first year at the school.

ABOVE: Barbara as a young woman, with her husband, William Powell. Circa 1965.

AT THE AGE OF NINETEEN, BARBARA INTERRUPTED her college education to marry Reverend William Holland Rowland Powell. They were married on January 1, 1955, and moved to Philadelphia. Barbara and her husband had four daughters and one son.

After settling down to raise her family, Barbara led no more protests and made no more speeches. She never sought fame or publicity for what she had done in 1951.

She finished her college education at Drexel University in Philadelphia, earning her bachelor's degree in library science in 1979. For twenty-four years Barbara worked as a librarian in the Philadelphia school district. Because she had always loved books and valued learning, she found her job deeply satisfying. As a school librarian, she could pass on the value of education to students in her district.

Barbara, her husband, and their daughters (left to right), Kelly, Tracy, Dawn, and Terry. 1978. Missing from the photo is their son, William Powell, Jr.

Barbara and Joan, who both settled down to raise families, often talked of missing their native county. Their family, after all, had lived in Prince Edward County for generations. That was where their roots went deep, so they wanted to see the family home rebuilt. Working closely with her sister and brothers, Barbara hired builders and oversaw the construction of a new structure on the site of the original house. She and her siblings planned to use the house for reunions and to maintain their ties to their childhood home county.

On September 25, 1991, shortly before the home was completed, Barbara died of cancer in Philadelphia. Those attending her funeral received a program bearing the words, "Nothing is so strong as gentleness, nothing so gentle as strength."

The Birth of the Civil Rights Movement

IN 1954, BARBARA'S FIERY AND OUTSPOKEN uncle, Reverend Vernon Johns, retired from his position as pastor of the Dexter Avenue Baptist Church in Montgomery, Alabama, and returned to his native Prince Edward County. His place as pastor of that congregation was taken by the twenty-five-year-old Martin Luther King Jr., who would become a leader in the civil rights movement.

The civil rights movement of the 1950s and 1960s aimed at ending racial discrimination in the United States. It largely consisted of peaceful marches, protests, boycotts, sit-ins, and voter registration drives. Peaceful protests advocating love and acceptance were a hallmark of the movement. Civil rights activists succeeded partly by creating widespread sympathy for the cause of racial equality and by attracting the attention of government leaders.

In 1955, Rosa Parks sparked the year-long massive Montgomery Bus Boycott when she refused to give up her seat to a white man on a segregated bus. The boycott succeeded in ending segregated buses in Montgomery, Alabama.

In 1957, as a result of the Montgomery Bus Boycott and a threatening phone call that particularly rattled him, Martin Luther King Jr. fully embraced nonviolence as a means of protest.

Barbara's idea of challenging government officials by means of a boycott to achieve racial equality was, in 1951, an innovative one. Previously, there had been labor strikes, which Barbara, an avid reader, would have known about. There had also been lawsuits challenging unfair conditions, acts of rebellion, and acts of civil disobedience in which citizens deliberately broke unjust laws. For example, in 1946 Irene Morgan had also been jailed for refusing to give up her seat on a bus. But Barbara's peaceful strike, intended to shut down a public institution to attain racial equality, was a novel idea at the time—and, for many of Barbara's contemporaries, a shocking and frightening one.

While Barbara's strike as a teenager in Prince Edward County, Virginia, did not unfold as she'd envisioned, the larger civil rights movement—encompassing the entire nation—did.

Some of the Moton High students who participated in the strike. 1953.

Author's Note

◇◇◇◇◇◇◇◇◇◇◇◇◇◇◇◇◇◇◇◇◇◇◇◇◇◇◇◇◇◇◇◇◇◇◇◇◇◇

I FIRST LEARNED ABOUT BARBARA ROSE JOHNS while reading Richard Kluger's book *Simple Justice*. I've always been drawn to stories about strong and innovative girls and young women, particularly those growing up in times and places that did not encourage them to be strong and innovative. For a teenager in 1951 to do what Barbara Johns did was astonishing. For a black teenager from a poor rural area in the segregated South in 1951 to do what she did was beyond astonishing. I knew immediately that I wanted to write a book about her.

As I came to know Barbara Johns through her writing and my interviews with her family and former classmates, she emerged as an engaging and likable person. One day, I was sitting with two of her brothers in the family home now rebuilt in Darlington Heights, struggling to get a feel for Barbara as a person and a leader. I said, "In her graduation picture, she seems so *sweet*." Ernest Johns, who always looked to his older sister as an authority figure, said, "Barbara was the *boss*." He had no trouble understanding why her classmates followed her out of the school: People did

A page from Barbara's own handwritten account of her childhood.

what his sister told them to do. It was that simple.

I asked why in later years she rarely talked about her strike and never sought recognition. "She did what she set out to do for her classmates and her race," Ernest Johns replied. "Her task was done."

Gathering the photographs for this book was a challenge. When the Johnses' house burned down in 1955, all the family photos were destroyed. Residents of a poor rural community generally did not own cameras. Major newspapers did not consider the strike important news, and participants and their families were frightened of possible conse-

IRENE TAYLOR
Barbara's close friend
MOTON HIGH
CLASS OF 1952

"When Barbara believed something wasn't right, she took matters very seriously."

JOHN WATSON
A strike leader with Barbara
MOTON HIGH
CLASS OF 1952

"During the planning, Barbara listened to suggestions, but more often than not, she'd already figured out the plan."

SAMUEL WILLIAMS
Senior class president
MOTON HIGH
CLASS OF 1952

"A lot of people who thought of Barbara as quiet and reserved were shocked by her speech [the day of the strike], but those of us who knew her, knew what she had in her."

CLAUDE COBBS
Barbara's future brother-in-law
MOTON HIGH
CLASS OF 1952

"What I remember most about Barbara is her beautiful smile and strong personality."

quences, so there are no photos of the strike itself. Even the 1951 yearbook—the source of many of the photos in this book—was of poor quality, reflecting Moton High School's inadequate funding.

In fact, for decades, nobody took an interest in Barbara's story. Her strike was rarely mentioned during the 1950s and '60s, even though *Brown v. Board of Education* was one of the century's most famous Supreme Court cases. Taylor Branch, Pulitzer Prize–winning author of *Parting the Waters: America in the King Years 1954–63*, suggested that its "schoolchild origins" were muffled because it was unheard of to credit a young girl with playing a major part in historical events.

The most unusual viewpoint comes from Ken Woodley, current editor of the *Farmville Herald*. Mr. Woodley frequently writes about Barbara and her legacy and proposed a local monument in her honor. During my visit with him in his office, we talked about how Barbara went into the woods to meditate. He startled me by saying, "Barbara Johns was a channel of grace."

Getting to know Barbara Rose Johns through my research has been a pleasure.

Writing this book and seeing it through to publication has been a privilege.

SELECT CIVIL RIGHTS TIMELINE

1868: THE FOURTEENTH AMENDMENT to the United States Constitution, requiring equal protection of the laws for all persons, is ratified.

1896: THE UNITED STATES Supreme Court decides *Plessy v. Ferguson*, holding that "separate but equal" facilities are constitutional.

1909: THE NATIONAL ASSOCIATION for the Advancement of Colored People (NAACP) is founded.

1935: THE NAACP BEGINS a legal campaign to challenge segregation in schools, beginning with graduate and professional schools on the theory that there would be less resistance to integrating schools for adults.

1951: BARBARA ROSE JOHNS leads her classmates out of Robert R. Moton High School in a peaceful strike to protest the unfair conditions at their school.

1954: THE SUPREME COURT decides *Brown v. Board of Education* and, reversing its decision in *Plessy v. Ferguson*, declares that school segregation is not equal and is unconstitutional.

1955: ROSA PARKS IS jailed for refusing to move to the back of a Montgomery, Alabama, bus. A peaceful boycott follows, resulting in the bus segregation ordinance being declared unconstitutional.

1957: ARKANSAS GOVERNOR ORVAL Faubus uses the National Guard to block nine black students from attending Little Rock High School. Following a court order, President Dwight Eisenhower sends in federal troops to allow the students to enter the school.

1960: FOUR BLACK COLLEGE students begin peaceful sit-ins at the lunch counter of a Greensboro, North Carolina, restaurant that refuses to serve black customers.

APRIL 16, 1963: DR. MARTIN LUTHER King Jr. is arrested and jailed during antisegregation protests in Birmingham, Alabama; he writes "Letter from a Birmingham Jail," arguing that individuals have a moral duty to disobey unjust laws.

AUGUST 28, 1963: ABOUT TWO HUNDRED thousand people join the March on Washington, D.C., congregating at the Lincoln Memorial, where Dr. King delivers his famous "I Have a Dream" speech.

SEPTEMBER 16, 1963: IN BIRMINGHAM, ALABAMA, four young black girls are killed while attending Sunday school when a bomb explodes at the Sixteenth Street Baptist Church, a popular location for civil rights meetings.

1964: PRESIDENT LYNDON B. JOHNSON signs the Civil Rights Act of 1964, which prohibits discrimination of all kinds based on race, color, religion, or national origin.

Page 4: "In the middle of the twentieth century . . . a leader arose among the black people." Richard Kluger, *Simple Justice*, p. 451.

Page 6: "I'm sick and tired" and "Why don't *you* do something about it?" Barbara's papers, p.14.

Page 9: "God, please. . . . We are your children, too." Barbara's papers, p. 16. Barbara described how she went to her favorite place in the woods with her horse to contemplate the problem of the tar paper shacks. She recorded the exact words of the prayers she uttered.

Page 10: "One morning in October . . ." Barbara's papers do not give the date or month of this incident. From other clues in her papers, and from dates I obtained from interviews with her former classmates, I concluded that this incident occurred in October.

Page 10: "Right then and there . . . didn't know what." Barbara's papers, p. 18.

Page 12: "As I lay in my bed . . . I hadn't been able to think of anything until then." Barbara's papers, p. 18.

Page 12: "The wolf also shall dwell . . . and a little child shall lead them." Kluger, *Simple Justice*, p. 467. Barbara used this quotation when talking about the strike with her classmates.

Page 14: "The ride on the train . . . as handsome as these men." Barbara's papers, p. 1.

Page 15: "She didn't have a lot of put-on airs . . . worrying about clothes." As quoted by Kluger, *Simple Justice*, p. 453.

Page 18: "Why are you calling him Uncle? He is not your uncle." As quoted by R. C. Smith, *They Closed Their Schools*, p. 29; also, author interview, Joan Johns Cobbs, October 9, 2010.

Page 19: "I roamed throughout the woods . . . quiet and peaceful." Barbara's papers, p. 4(a).

Page 20: "They, too, were tired of attending school in tar paper shacks." Kluger, *Simple Justice*, p. 467, and author interview, John Watson, November 9, 2010.

Page 21: "Barbara told me the plan. . . . It was shocking." Author interview, Edwilda Allen, September 4, 2010.

Page 21: "Complete secrecy was vital." While all the students, including Barbara in her diaries, insist that no adults were involved in the planning of the strike, Miss Inez Davenport, in recent interviews, said that Barbara secretly consulted with her during the planning stages and that Barbara was sworn to secrecy.

Page 24: "Are we going to just accept . . . or are we going to do something about it?" Author interview, Irene Taylor McVay, November 19, 2010.

Page 24: "After that speech, *everyone* knew who she was." Author interview, Rev. J. Samuel Williams, October 10, 2010.

Page 24: "She put into words . . . the courage to stand up and say it." Author interview, Joy Cabarrus Speakes, April 25, 2011.

Page 24: "The jail isn't big enough for all of us." Author interview, John Watson, November 9, 2010. Also from Kluger, *Simple Justice*, pp. 468 and 476.

Page 26: "After the meeting . . . Barbara called the NAACP . . . to help the students." Oliver Hill, who took the phone call, always insisted that the caller was Barbara. R. C. Smith, author of *They Closed Their Schools*, interviewed Barbara on January 26, 1961. During this interview, Barbara's memory was not clear on this point, and she couldn't remember the phone call. School records, however, show that the phone call was made from the school to the NAACP office in Richmond on that Monday.

Page 26: The full text of this letter was reprinted in Kluger, *Simple Justice*, p. 467.

Page 27: "I'm not surprised by anything Barbara does." Smith, *They Closed Their Schools,* p. 53, quoting Barbara, who, in a letter dated May 11, 1960, described what her father said.

Page 27: "Grandma, I walked out of school this morning. . . . Stick with us." As quoted by Kluger, *Simple Justice*, p. 471.

Page 29: "put-up job." Kluger, *Simple Justice*, p. 469. Inez Davenport Jones, who knew the students well, said, "Nobody told those students what to say." Author interview, April 4, 2011.

Page 30: "We'd like to help you fellas . . . blow his brains out." Anecdote, including direct quotes, from Kluger, *Simple Justice*, p. 476.

Page 30: "We will stay out of school indefinitely. . . . No jail is big enough for all of us." From Kluger, *Simple Justice*, p. 476, drawing on his interview with Oliver Hill.

Page 32: "The problem is that a new colored high school . . . must not be allowed to continue." *Richmond Afro-American*, "No Toms Can Stop Us," May 12, 1951.

Page 32: "We met whatever obstacle we were given, no matter how difficult." Author interview, John Watson, November 9, 2010.

Page 32: "Ill advised," and "student-inspired mass hookie." *Farmville Herald*, Editorial page, April 27, 1951.

Page 34: "They all came out together . . . stop you from backing us." Direct quotes and summary from *Richmond Afro-American*, "No Toms Can Stop Us."

Page 34: "Don't let any Tom, Dick, or Harry Pervall stop you from supporting us." Author interview, Joan Johns Cobbs. Ms. Cobbs distinctly remembered Barbara saying this as well, so I included this quotation as well as the quotation from the newspaper article.

Page 35: "little girl . . . unafraid to speak her mind." *Richmond Afro-American*, "No Toms Can Stop Us."

Page 35: "Anyone who would not back these children . . . is not a man." *Richmond Afro-American*, "No Toms Can Stop Us."

Page 38: "Barbara was so excited, she shouted with happiness." Author interview, Joan Johns Cobbs, October 9, 2010.

Page 45: "Barbara was the boss . . . her task was done." Author interview, Ernest Johns, April 23, 2011.

Page 46: "schoolchild origins." Taylor Branch, *Parting the Waters: America in the King Years 1954–63*, p. 21.

Page 46: "Barbara Johns was a channel of grace." Author interview, Ken Woodley, October 10, 2010.

Page 46: "When Barbara believed . . . took matters very seriously." Author interview, Irene Taylor McVay, November 19, 2010.

Page 46: "During the planning, . . . already figured out the plan." Author interview, John Watson, April 9, 2012.

Page 46: "A lot of people . . . knew what she had in her." Author interview, Rev. J. Samuel Williams, October 10, 2010.

Page 46: "What I remember most . . . beautiful smile and strong personality." Author interview, Claude Cobbs, April 23, 2011.

SOURCES

The most important sources were Barbara's own hand-written papers, my interviews with her family and former classmates, and the books and documentaries listed below, which in turn relied on original sources. Where I found discrepancies, I used my judgment in resolving them. In one instance, I found numerous differences between a published memoir and other eyewitness accounts, so I omitted that memoir from this list.

BARBARA'S PAPERS / HANDWRITTEN MEMOIR

Johns, Barbara Rose, handwritten memoir, courtesy of the Moton Museum and Powell family.

BOOKS AND QUARTERLIES

Branch, Taylor. *Parting the Waters: America in the King Years 1954–63.* New York: Simon and Schuster, 1988.

Kluger, Richard. *Simple Justice.* New York: Vintage, 1975.

Smith, R. C. "Prince Edward County: Revisited and Revitalized." *The Virginia Quarterly Review*, Vol. 73, Number 1. Winter 1997.

Smith, R. C. *They Closed Their Schools.* Chapel Hill: University of North Carolina Press, 1965.

Steck, John C. *The Prince Edward County, Virginia Story.* Published by the *Farmville Herald*, Farmville, VA, 1960.

Turner, Kara Miles. "Both Victors and Victims: Prince Edward County, Virginia, the NAACP, and *Brown*." *Virginia Law Review*, Vol. 90:1667, 2004.

DOCUMENTARIES

Farmville: An American Story. Quest Videolines Productions. 2002. Bill Jersey and Richard Wormser.

The Ground Beneath Our Feet: Virginia's History Since the Civil War: Massive Resistance. 1998. George H. Gilliam and William G. Thomas III.

AUTHOR INTERVIEWS

Allen, Edwilda, former Moton High student. September 4, 2010; February 2, 2011; April 23, 2011.

Cobbs, Claude, Barbara's brother-in-law. April 22, 2011; April 23, 2011.

Cobbs, Joan Johns, Barbara's sister. September 28, 2010; October 9, 2010; October 10, 2010; November 9, 2010; February 12, 2011; April 23, 2011; April 25, 2011.

Jackson, Marie, former Moton High student and longtime resident of Farmville. April 22, 2011.

Johns, Ernest, Barbara's brother. October 9, 2010; April 23, 2011.

Johns, Robert, Barbara's brother. April 23, 2011.

Johns, Roderick, Barbara's brother. October 9, 2010; April 23, 2011.

Jones, Inez Davenport, Barbara's favorite teacher. April 4, 2011; April 23, 2011.

McVay, Irene Taylor, former Moton High student and close friend of Barbara's. November 19, 2010.

Shepperson, Willie, former Moton High student. April 22, 2011.

Smith, R. C., author of *They Closed Their Schools.* April 15, 2011.

Speakes, Joy Cabarrus, former Moton High student. April 22, 2011; April 25, 2011.

Stokes, John, former Moton High student. November 9, 2010.

Taylor, Charlie, former Moton High student, born and raised in Farmville. April 22, 2011.

Walker, Rosalie, Darlington Heights resident, grew up on a dairy farm five miles from the Johns family, friend of Barbara's. April 25, 2011.

Wallenstein, Peter, professor of history, Virginia Tech. April 22, 2011.

Watson, John, former Moton High student. November 9, 2010; February 17, 2011; April 9, 2012.

Williams, Rev. J. Samuel, former Moton High student, 1952 senior class president. October 10, 2010.

Woodley, Ken, editor of the *Farmville Herald*. October 10, 2010.

OTHER INTERVIEWS

Allen, Edwilda. Interview by George Gilliam, for the documentary *The Ground Beneath Our Feet*. 2000.

Allen, Vera Jones. Interview by George Gilliam, for the documentary *The Ground Beneath Our Feet*, 2000.

Cobbs, Joan Johns. Interview, Congress of Racial Equality. July 30, 2009.

Hill, Oliver. Interview by George Gilliam, for the documentary *The Ground Beneath Our Feet*. 2000.

NEWSPAPER ARTICLES AND EDITORIALS

Farmville Herald: "Ill Advised Move," Editorial page, April 27, 1951.

Farmville Herald: "School Days or Happy Days," Letter to the Editor, April 27, 1951.

Richmond Afro-American: "Cross Burning in Farmville Kept Close Secret," May 8, 1951.

Richmond Afro-American: "No Toms Can Stop Us: Pupil Lashes Out at School Principal," May 12, 1951.

Richmond Afro-American: "Va. Pupils' Strike Ends," May 12, 1951.

IMAGE CREDITS

The paper background texture used throughout the book is by Dustin Schmieding.

Page 5, top: Courtesy of the Afro-American Newspapers Archives and Research Center

Page 5, bottom: Courtesy of Edwilda Allen

Page 6: National Archives

Page 7, top left: National Archives

Page 7, top right: Courtesy of Spellman College

Page 7, bottom left: National Archives

Page 7, bottom right: Courtesy of Inez Davenport Jones

Page 9, top left: Author's collection

Page 9, bottom left: Author's collection

Page 9, right: Courtesy of the Johns family

Page 10, top: Courtesy of the Johns family

Page 10, bottom: Author's collection

Page 11: From the Robert R. Moton High School 1951 Yearbook, courtesy of John Watson

Page 12: From the Robert R. Moton High School 1951 Yearbook, courtesy of John Watson

Page 13: Courtesy of Richard McClintock

Page 14, top and bottom: Courtesy of the Johns family

Page 15, top: Author's collection

Page 15, bottom: Courtesy of the Hampden-Sydney College Photograph Archives

Page 16: Courtesy of the Moorland-Spingarn Research Center, Howard University

Page 17, from left: TM & © 2014 Archie Comic Publications, Inc. Used with permission; Courtesy of Random House, Inc.; Permission granted by HarperCollins Publishers; public domain

Page 18: Courtesy of Bob Flippen, Proprietor, Southside Virginia Historical Press

Page 19: From the Robert R. Moton High School 1951 Yearbook, courtesy of John Watson

Page 20, top and bottom: National Archives

Page 21, left: Courtesy of Edwilda Allen

Page 21, right: Courtesy of Inez Davenport Jones

Page 23: National Archives

Page 25, left: Compliments of the Virginia State Conference NAACP Photograph Archives

Page 25, right: Author's collection

Page 27: National Archives

Page 28, top left: From the Robert R. Moton High School 1951 Yearbook, courtesy of John Watson

Page 28, top right: Courtesy of Ken Woodley

Page 28, bottom: Courtesy of the Farmville-Prince Edward County Historical Society

Page 30: Courtesy of the Afro-American Newspapers Archives and Research Center

Page 31: Time & Life Pictures

Page 32: Compliments of the Virginia State Conference NAACP Photograph Archives

Pages 33 and 34: Courtesy of the Afro-American Newspapers Archives and Research Center

Page 36: Courtesy of the Johns family

Page 37, top: Courtesy of Spelman College

Page 37, bottom: NAACP Collection, Prints and Photographs Division, Library of Congress

Page 39: Courtesy of the Fuqua School, Farmville, VA

Pages 41 and 42: Courtesy of the Johns and Powell families

Page 44: Time & Life Pictures/Getty Images

Page 45: Courtesy of the Powell family and the Moton Museum, Farmville, VA

Page 46, all images: From the Robert R. Moton High School 1951 Yearbook, courtesy of John Watson

ACKNOWLEDGMENTS

THIS BOOK COULD NOT HAVE BEEN WRITTEN without the generosity of those who shared their time, their memories, and, in many cases, their personal photographs: Edwilda Allen, Claude Cobbs, Terry Powell Harrison, Marie Jackson, Ernest Johns, Robert Johns, Roderick Johns, Inez Davenport Jones, Irene Taylor McVay, Joy Cabarrus Speakes, Charlie Taylor, Rosalie Walker, John Watson, Rev. J. Samuel Williams, and Ken Woodley. Particular thanks to Joan Johns Cobbs, who read my drafts for accuracy. Any errors, of course, are my own.

Thanks also to the librarians, archivists, and professors throughout Virginia who aided my research and provided historical information: Patrice Carter at the Moton Museum in Farmville, Leslie Jo Andrews at the Fuqua School in Farmville, Lydia Williams and Ruth Gowin at the Longwood University Library, Richard McClintock at Hampden-Sydney College, Robin Sedgewick at the Longwood Center for Visual Arts, Susan Bagby at Longwood University, Dale Neighbors at the Library of Virginia, and Bret Peaden at the Hampden-Sydney College Library. Thanks to Professor Peter Wallenstein at Virginia Tech University for help with local history.

Special thanks to my editor, Howard Reeves, whose creative vision shaped this book; Maria Middleton, for her superb book design; managing editor Jen Graham, for making sure every *i* was dotted and every *t* crossed; production manager Alison Gervais, for ensuring that the entire book looked beautiful; Sabrina Schloss, for her Photoshop expertise; Betsy Wattenberg, friend and critic beyond compare; and Andy Schloss, for everything.

INDEX